Constellations of You

Mackenzie Miller

BookLeaf
Publishing

Presentation by *BookLeaf Publishing*

Web: www.bookleafpub.com

E-mail: info@bookleafpub.com

ISBN: 9789358312416

First edition 2023

Dedication: To my friends & family, thank you for loving me & shaping me into the person I am. To Brooke, I appreciate your constant support in healing, expression, & so much more. Thank you. To everyone I lost along the way, I hope you're healing too.

PREFACE

Content warning: Sexual assault, abuse
For those reading on various mental health journeys, please be mindful of your own triggers & wellbeing while reading. If you are not up to reading about certain topics, please prioritize yourself first

Colors of You

I was a victim then a villain,
Now I'm nowhere in between.
I am lost, left misguided,
By who you tried to make me be.
Started out as a prize of gold
Then you dropped me between the cracks.
You called me family
Then abused me,
Unlike the parents I was blessed with.
You thought you won me
Like all the trophies I won for you.
In the end,
You chose a bully & black sheep
But all you got was one less kid
To push around.

I now hate the color purple
Cause it takes me back to you.
Just a crayon or a sharpie,
Feels unsafe within my grasp.
You colored our secrets with shades
That used to be my favorite.
Now my bedroom walls are coated
In reminders of your malice.
Sometimes when I wake in

The middle of the night,
I see your face in the paint,
Looming closer & closer
To my paralyzed sleep state.
I thought closing my eyes
Would make you disappear,
But you linger behind my eyelids.

When I enter an unfamiliar space,
The first thing I do is explore,
Searching the mirrors for cameras
& corners for your hidden spies.
The tools you use to watch
& take note of how to prey upon
Children who just want you to love them.
Your favorite hobbies are illegal
Guess that's why our time ran out.
Voice recognition & speech translation
On kids who are too afraid to speak up.
I'm stuck with trauma, never ending,
But at least depressions better
Than you ever were.

I've kept secrets,
Upheld lies,
Protecting you,
People who were supposed to keep me safe,
People who never tried to protect me.
Or maybe you did try,

In the beginning,
But your unlawful urges got the best of you.
I'm done hiding the truth,
From myself & from the world.

I have risen above & overcome &
Been the bigger person.
As a child,
I was the bigger person.
Someone should've told me:
Being the bigger person hurts more.
Being the bigger person doesn't heal you.

Easter

You picked me up
On the evening of Easter,
In your shitty silver car
With the crowded bumper stickers
On the trunk.
We had plans for a picnic
The next day in the park,
But we just couldn't wait
Even 24 hours longer.
You handed me the aux cord
& drove around looking
For a place to park
& admire the stars.

Flying over the curb
Of a neighborhood that
Had since gone to bed,
We crawled out of the car,
Leaving it parked behind the chain
As we ducked into the
Eerily lit construction zone.
The no trespassing sign
Reflected the headlights
Back into our excited eyes
& rules I usually obeyed

Suddenly didn't matter.

We laughed the whole way up
This huge pile of dirt,
You climbing first &
Telling me to watch my step.
At the top, the sky was clear
& the stars seemed a little brighter
Than the night before.
There we layed,
Side by side,
Barely touching until it got
Far too cold to be out in the wind.

Walking back to the car
Was hardly easy at all,
More so the two of us
Stumbling down the mound
We once climbed.
My throat was dry
From talking so much,
But I didn't mind.
My converse, once white,
Were stained with grass & mud
& cherished memories,
But I didn't mind.

Complicated

It's complicated.
He didn't mean to hurt me.
His intentions weren't bad.
I'm probably being dramatic.

I used to think that what
Happened between
Us was complicated,
Too complicated to
Try to untangle or
Piece back together
The puzzle that is
My forgotten memories.
But pieces are fractured & damaged
Or missing all together,
Left incomplete in a notebook
I threw in the trash.

I used to tell people that
What happened between
Us was complicated.
No one wrote me
An instruction manual
Of how to proceed
After you & that moment

& that basement.

He didn't ask me
If i was comfortable
With his weight
On top of mine,
Our bare skin touching
In places i thought
Belonged to me.

He didn't stop going
Or feeling
Or kissing
Or grabbing,
When I laid motionless,
Unable to move
Or speak
Or be present
In my own body.

Consent isn't complicated.
Consent isn't one & done.
Consent isn't coercion.
Consent isn't manipulation.
Consent isn't complicated.

Madds

I miss when we were kids,
Making potions in our bubble wands,
My head in your lap as
I fall asleep during
Christmas church mass,
The choir singing a glorious
But pitchy rendition of silent night.
I miss when we played together,
When you'd correct my errors
In pretend school before we
Discovered we disliked it.

I miss when you taught me things,
Going behind our parents backs
To teach me to read at age four
& helping me shoot baskets
In our driveway.
Even if I hit you too many times
With my incompetent basketball skills
Or broke a few fingers playing defense,
You were never mad at me.
You just laughed it off the same way
That you do now as an adult.

I miss the way you used to take care of me,

Feeding me skittles when I had a tick
& holding my hand to get my ears pierced.
You still look after me today,
Just different now that I'm grown;
Going first when we pierced our noses,
Driving me to the gas station for
11pm slushy nights,
& cheering me on at college,
Even over facetime,
Thousands of miles apart.

Different Now

If you touch upon me for too long,
Even hesitate upon my skin,
You'll leave a bruise.
You can't always see it,
But I know it's there.
Where your hands laid,
I feel an indentation,
Part of your soul reaching in
To grab at my insides with
The same greediness
You've always possessed.

Things are different now,
Or at least they should be.
You took yourself far, far away
From the dire history we wrote here
& I guess I did too.
Your body is gone now.
Your voice is too,
Your vindictive composure
Along with them.
I may not remember every detail
From that night but I can't just
Forget it like you did.

I can still feel your hot breath
In my ear as you whisper to me,
The movie still playing behind us.
My body still cringes at the thought
Of your words touching my neck.

I still feel nauseated when I
Picture myself willingly walk
Down that staircase with you,
Hearing you shut the door
After I passed, as if
Guiding me into hell
Made you a gentleman.

I still feel embarrassed,
Ashamed of what I let you do.
When I recall staring in the mirror
At a teary-eyed person I didn't recognize,
My neck covered in bruises I didn't
Find pleasure in receiving.

Things are supposed to be different now.
They're supposed to feel different now.
But they don't.
I'm still plagued by the marks
You left black & blue on my body.
Worse are the black & gray on my brain,
The black & gray on my heart.

Easier to Love

If I only knew your patterns of migration,
Fluctuating temper of cool to steaming,
I'd have thought you to be a butterfly.
You started out tame & frail,
People pleasing & caring for students,
Bright & happy with stars in their eyes
& dreams yet to be crushed.
You called me family, the star student,
A wonderful & kind child.

You evolved,
Changed values & ethics,
Going after my family & more,
As if malevolence carried you
Towards a bounty reward.
You threw knives at my chest;
A perplexing betrayal struck me
Not knowing why I was a target.
I didn't realize you were envious,
Of not my skills or strengths
But of my kindness & compassion.
Because even you knew, I could
Never lose empathy for you.

I changed.

You changed.
But did I really change, or
Did I used to be easier to love?

Dear Younger Me

Someday you will learn
That you have a voice,
A unique one, &
You are capable of speaking your
Truth without paralyzing concerns
Of others' perception.
Even when the words crawl up
Through your lungs & become
Tangled in your throat,
You will find a source of safe expression
To outline those thoughts in ink.

Someday you will learn to
Till your own cup up first,
To repair your broken pieces
Before acting as a lifeline
To everyone else.
You don't owe anyone your
Time or your energy,
Your smile or your comfort.
You do, however, owe that care
& attention to yourself.

Someday you will learn to
Let go of the boulders

Weighing you down &
Release the grueling pain
You carry within.
Without the fog,
You'll feel grateful for the
Sun's smiling warmth & the
Light bounce in your step.
A year of freedom is much better
Than a lifetime unable to breathe.

Someday you will learn to
Set boundaries & protect
Your inner peace,
No longer feeling guilty for
Knowing & respecting your worth.
Saying "no" is not rude or a
Language to be punished,
Not selfish or cold,
Not inconsiderate or unkind.
Saying "no" means listening to yourself
& honoring your needs.

Someday you will learn to
Tear down the brick walls
Around your heart,
To find power in vulnerability,
& allow people to love you unconditionally.
Early on, some will chip away at your light
& blow out your flame,

But my dear,
It is only temporary;
Your fire will ignite again,
Standing brighter & bolder than before.

Someday you will learn
To fight back against being
Bullied, abused, ridiculed.
You'll forgive both them & yourself,
Acknowledging your right to live
Free from the pain that they caused.
You will reconnect with your freedom of choice
Deciding to take it back fiercely &
wholeheartedly.

Someday you will learn that
Recovery is a choice,
A heart racing,
Head pounding decision
That lies within your small, tired hands.
You did not choose to endure years
Of mistreatment and malice,
Though it is your responsibility to heal
From people & places you no longer speak of.
Recovery is a difficult road that
You are more than capable of traveling.

Someday you will learn that
You matter;

Regardless of your body size or weight,
Your productivity or grades,
You are beyond worthy.
You'll laugh, reflecting on years
When bitter souls convinced you otherwise.
You will no longer view their opinions as
True facts but objective opinions that
Do not define you.

Someday you will learn that
You have a purpose.
You are meant to be here:
Here in this room, in this life, on this earth.
You are not meant to just exist or survive
But to truly and authentically live.

Everything I Want to Say

I want to say i'm sorry
For the way that you grew up.
A middle child
Who never learned
To raise herself up
Without pinning others down.
I want to say i'm sorry
For how things changed between us.
Maybe, if we would've been safe,
Our anxieties & insecurities wouldn't
Have ripped us apart.
I want to say i'm sorry
For allowing you to stab me in the back
Over & over with no remorse or apology
Or promise to stop adding
Weights to my chest.
I fear I taught you that
Bullying your best friend was okay.

I realize now that my apology
Doesn't mean you're sorry too.
You ridiculed me in the middle of class
For seeing a therapist at age thirteen,
Then decided on the psych field
As your fancy helping career.

You laughed about my weight
When we were only twelve.
The car ride home,
I took a pair of scissors to my arm,
The first time I punished my body for not living
Up to other people's expectations.
That night, I wrapped my undeserving body
In plastic wrap while I slept,
With hopes that the next day,
You'd take back the things you said.
But you never did,
Only added to the list of reasons
Why I was inferior to you.

I know i'm ugly
Because you told me so.
For years you pushed me
From every photo,
Every instagram post
Because I'm not "photogenic"
In the same way you were.
You planted the seed
& i'm still digging & digging,
Trying to uproot the invasion
Of your words in my brain.

So I guess in the end,
This apology isn't to you.

It's to me.
These are the memories,
The words, I never got to say,
The ones I hid from everyone,
Including myself.

Playing with Fire

When you said you'd be my truest friend,
This isn't how I thought we'd end.
Maybe it's cause you were 42
& I could barely tie my shoes.
You had a wife, 2 kids, for all to see,
But your profile picture was of you & me.
You didn't really have a plan,
Just used the power of your hand
To fan my flame when it burned out
Then watched me melt & hurt myself.

Time after time,
Part of me refuses to learn.
You've infused evil in my brain
That travels through my bloodstream,
Dismantling protections & progress.
Because somehow, I still see the best in people,
Even after suffering the worst of intentions.
In the end, I'm still the same little kid,
Longing to be seen & heard,
Falling for the person who gave it to me.

I should have listened when my parents told me
not to play with fire.

Forgiveness

To the people who hurt me,

I forgive you.
Not because I want to.
Not because you deserve it.
Because I deserve it.

I forgive you-
For the unspeakable words you ingrained in my
mind;
The ones that told me I was not enough.
The ones that shattered my self-worth little by
little.
The ones that convinced me I was undeserving
of love.
The ones that sickened me until it was almost
too late.
Maybe the seed of hopelessness had already
been planted,
But you watered it,
Allowing it to grow & poison the flowers around
it.
You, someone I trusted & looked up to, did a lot
of damage.

You, someone who said they loved me, hurt me
as if you didn't.

I forgive you-
For the memories that replay through my head
over & over again.
The ones that feel so real, I can hear your voice;
My body trembling as I relive your abuse.
The ones I can see in my sleep;
So vivid I feel your threatening presence in my
room.
The ones that chain me tightly to the past;
Unable to live freely in the present.

I forgive you-
For taking advantage of me & stealing my
childhood.
Sure, I was broken when you found me,
But one small fracture was enough.
Enough vulnerability for you to swoop in &
make more.
I sometimes confused the tape & glue you used,
To hold all my pieces together as support.
When really, it was just the calm before the
storm;
The peace before your tornado of destruction,
Tore me limb from limb once more.

I forgive you-

For encouraging my pre-existing habits;
The ones that shrank me down & made me
smaller.
The ones that left my body covered in scars.
& most importantly, the ones that opened
Invisible wounds in my mind,
That I have since learned to stitch back together.

Sure, I could continue down a path I once
walked;
A dark & lonely road built on lies,
Leading to a lifetime of make-believe.
You pretending you didn't hurt me,
& me being dragged along behind you.
But that is not the life I want for myself,
Not anymore.
It took until recently to understand this.
The experiences & trauma I endured were
validated,
Reassuring that it was not my fault.
I did not ask for it to happen.
Then, realizing my trauma does not define me.
I didn't have to live that way forever;
Repeating negative cycles,
Believing I didn't deserve to be alive.
So now that I forgave myself for what you did,
Allowing myself to be hurt & poorly treated,
I forgive you.

I forgive you.
Not because I want to.
Not because you deserve it.
Because I deserve it.
I deserve a life free from the pain you caused.

Between Sidewalk Squares

Blissful memories sprout
Through my broken &
Cracked skin as the
Delicate flowers do,
The ones that blossom
Between sidewalk squares.

Taking walks to through corn fields
To visit the old school house,
Just up the road from your house.
Your welcoming home scented with
Freshly brewed mint tea &
Chimes of the grandfather clock.
Building fairy gardens to pass time,
My forever, favorite indulgence,
Sat right beneath the trees at the lake.
You moved furniture, small berries,
Thimbles, & buttons around the
Town we built,
Just to make me smile.
Playing the the creek,
Trying to catch insects, not spiders,
Picking apples for a sweet snack.

Climbing the old, twisted tree

At the fence of your backyard,
The one with the swing I used
To boost me up in the air.
Playing barber shop with pink
Scissors & smocks,
Too dull to cut hair.
Removing drawers kept
Under our uncle's bed,
Creating a hidden space just as
Tiny & reserved as I was.
Painting horses from memory,
You cheering me on as if I
Were Picasso at only age eight.

Amongst the weeds
They grow small, however,
The beauty is always there
If you look for it.

Without an Apology

You asked me why I was quiet.
You begged me to confess.
You pleaded for an inside scoop
Of the dialogue running through my mind,
Distracting me from care & trust
& authentic human connection.

You smiled softly &
Embraced me slowly,
Shielding your villainous eyes
That couldn't conceal your
Intention to fuel the fire
With my vulnerability.

You taught me to hide myself away,
Pack my truth in an overflowing suitcase
With the belittling words you whispered
& the emotions I disconnected from.
You taught me that I was undeserving
Of protection from the abuse you
Watched overtake me, by caring more
About how your boyfriend's parents perceive
you
Than my security & wellbeing.
You taught me that as long as I was

Winning trophies or getting scholarships,
I was functioning enough to withstand
Traumas I shouldn't have had to.

You were a good teacher,
One of my favorites.
You just taught me all the wrong things.
You taught me that accepting abuse
From someone who said they
Loved you was normal.
& after all this time,
I still have love left for you.

Six months after releasing
My fear & anger into this poem,
I forgive you.
I forgive you for what you did,
& what you didn't do,
Not the apology I never received.
I wasn't ready before.
I am now.

Life Jacket

I needed a life jacket.
I knew how to swim ever since I was three or
four.
It came naturally to me; never crying for help
Or demanding that my parents hold me.
The praise & attention I received,
I could never quite understand.
Sure, I didn't wear arm floaties or
Tightly hold on to the rope like other kids my
age,
But all I did was keep my head above the water.

What's so special about surviving?
Weren't we made to easily keep ourselves alive?
I rarely noticed the protection that my friends
received
When they couldn't swim for even a few
seconds
Without being pulled underwater.
I didn't understand why caution & lifesavers
were necessary.
I guess a girl who smiled bright &
Wasn't afraid to swim too far,
Didn't look like someone who would
Eventually need a life jacket.

Most children feared the deep end,
Where they could no longer stand,
But the dark & empty side of the pool never
scared me.
I may have been small & alone,
But I swam ahead anyway.

As I grew up,
I continued to keep my head above the water.
Sometimes, the waves came out of nowhere
& shoved me backwards,
But I always made it to the shore safely.
Things were different from when I was younger
though.
I was different.
I had seen too many shipwrecks
& weathered more storms than imaginable for a
teenager.
The serene pool of comfort I had once been
supported by
Disappeared before I recognized it was gone.
I kept moving forward,
Engaging my already weak & broken body in a
rocky ocean,
With waves determined to pin me below the
surface.
Though people observing my growth watched
me dive in confidently,
I was barely treading water.

They couldn't see my legs growing tired
Or the mountainous roadblocks my mind had
created.
No one noticed me shivering in open waters
Or my lungs desperate for sufficient air.

I slipped too deep,
Discovering dangerous waters that have
Taken the lives of many people like me.
One too many times,
I was caught in a seemingly never ending
current of affliction,
My hope to reach land withering away each
time.
My mind had poisoned my body as
It was longing for rest I was unable to supply.
I gave up.

Then, there was you.
My life jacket.
Your bright & airy essence
Pulled me from somewhere deeper, darker, &
lonelier
Than the deep end I once experienced.
I was unsure of your guidance;
Preferring to drown than to fight.
I was beyond prepared for water to fill my lungs,
Making my body too heavy to float.
I never learned to use the rescue whistle

To send my plea for help.

Maybe,
I wouldn't have been brave enough
To surrender, even if I had.
You didn't just swoop in to grab me &
Drag my body to shore,
Then leave me on my own,
Like lifeguards on tv.
Sure, it would've kept me alive a little longer,
But your confidence in my ability to
Save my own life carried me on.
You filled my lungs with air &
Kept me afloat until my strength returned.

I'm not sure what I did
To deserve your presence,
But today, I couldn't be more grateful for it.
You taught me how to swim again.
Maybe the most difficult part wasn't moving
My arms & legs in the proper motion,
But reminding me I deserved to be saved.

Now, I swim alone;
A little shaky at times but the
Worthiness of survival you instilled in me
Gave me the courage to face harsh waves.
You are saving others like me,
The promising souls who wish to drown.

& I no longer need a life jacket,
But sometimes when I'm tired,
I miss the warmth & safety of your embrace.
It's nice to know you'll always be there
If I start to sink, watching me with pride
As I save myself.

Lego Keychains

I've never had people,
Friends, that care so much about me.
Friends who call me when I'm alone,
Reassure me when I'm unsafe,
Walk me across the empty
Parking lot to my car,
Watching as I drive away.

I found safety.
Safety is you.

I've never had friends
Who celebrated my victories,
Both big & small,
Like their own.
Whether it's staying clean
Or making my bed,
I'm never left alone,
Only reminded to be proud of myself,
The way you're proud of me.

I found authenticity.
Authenticity is you.

I've rarely experienced

Days of pure happiness,
Unclouded by the paralysis
Of mind body disconnection.
Thanks to your mindless jokes &
Perfectly crafted compliments,
I come face to face with
An abundance of joy more frequently
Than I ever have before.

Yesterday, you created another of these days.
You charmed me with liquid sunshine,
Even with storms appearing in the sky.
I was laughing so hard I believed
I would stop breathing,
My cheeks burning from
Pulling into a smile so much.
Lego keychains that connect us
Even when we're miles apart,
I'm grateful for any reminder
Of my love & trust in you.

I found happiness.
Happiness is you.

Lucky You

I think I loved you once.
Or maybe, I just don't
Know what love is,
Distorted visions of adoration
Subjecting me to false acquisitions.
It's knocked at my door
A few times in the past,
But I always left it waiting,
In fear that I'd scare it away.

That's how you liked it though, right?
You found amusement in
The game of our relationship,
You holding the rule book & me
Desperate for your deceitful validation.
You took pleasure in playing
The board game of my body,
Without a nod or whisper of consent.
Or maybe you liked the thrill,
The adventure, the risk that I brought;
You didn't actually love me
Like I thought you did,
Like you said you did.

Can you have love without honesty?

Without friendship? WIthout trust?
It's not your fault I guess,
Taking advantage of someone
Who was far too damaged
To know why you were misleading her.
You didn't make me this way,
Wire my brain with faulty programming.
You just saw me headed your direction
& chose to roll the dice of chance.
Lucky you, lucky you,
You win again &
I lost the game I never
Even knew I was playing.

Notes App Message

You're sorry? Really?
You're sorry now?
Your apology is a manuscript
Of your guilt and selfishness,
Asking me for forgiveness
So you can move on to the next girl
& feel better about everything you've done.

This apology isn't for me,
It's for yourself.
You want closure because
Of the gut-wrenching feeling,
Not that you acted inhuman,
But that someone might found out
& treat you differently than before.

You can't come to me
Dictating a decision about closure
Based on what you want.
It's always been about what you want
& I've played along with a smile.
You don't have that power,
Or any power, in my life anymore.
I've given myself closure by challenging
Thoughts that do not define me.

You said it yourself;
Your apologies mean nothing to me,
Not because I'm angry at you,
But because I have worked towards healing.
You acknowledge that your sad excuse of an
apology
Registers as empty to me,
Yet you keep apologizing anyway.
I won't tell you it's okay because it isn't.
Either way, it's not my forgiveness that you
need.
It's your own.

Since I've Seen You

Since i've seen you,
Felt you,
Been burned by you,
So many things are different:
Me, my passions, my talents,
My bravery in using my voice.

Since i've seen you,
I've gotten a new phone,
One without your number
embedded inside.
I've chopped my hair to my chin,
more than once,
& dyed it red, pink, & rose gold.
I've made new friends that don't
Ridicule my every move,
Lost a few,
Gained some more.

I've broken up with my boyfriend
& found peace in being single,
Enjoying my own company.
I've tried to end my life
& found a new outlook of living.
I've come out as queer

& graduated high school
& moved 6 hours away.

I don't know you anymore.
I'm glad that I don't.
I still think about you on your birthday,
holidays we spent together.

I don't know you anymore.
I hope you've changed.
Somehow, my gut wretches at the thought,
Telling me that you haven't.
Haven't grown or changed or
Improved your behavior.

I don't know if you're ignorant & clueless,
Or if you understand
The laws you're breaking
& don't care about those you hurt.
Maybe I'm better off not knowing.

The pain you inflict
On poor children who aren't
Old enough to know better
Makes its way back to me,
Calling out, not to bring me down,
But you remind me how privileged
I am to never have to see you again.

You don't know me anymore.
Yet at the same time,
I am exactly the same.
My fear of you is less
But still ever present.
Because when abuse happens,
Your biggest fear is the
Constant threat of believing
It will happen to you again.
I'm not unhealed but healing.

Jillian

We used to draw cats on our wrists,
Black & pink sharpie, tattooed young skin,
So we'd always be together.
Chasing each other around middle school
bathrooms,
Laughing & playing like children
For what seemed like the first & last time.
Facetiming for hours,
Through fevers & breakups;
Slaying dragons both imaginary & real.

I think it's cute,
The way you bounce lightly
On your toes while you walk
& how you nurture every being
Who walks amongst your path.
You are composed with humility,
So much so, you can hardly see
What a genuine gift you are
To the world.
To my world.

No amount of hand-written letters or birthday
cards,
Sticky note drawings nor text messages,

Are enough to capture my lyrics
Of love from me to you.

45

I never fought alone,
Not without a hug or kiss on the cheek,
Or birthday cake m&m's from last halloween.
Kissing each other to make our boyfriends mad
& keeping each other alive another day longer.
No secret too embarrassing to tell
& no tears too many to shed.
Where would I be without your unconditional
love
Imprinted within my soul?
I'm not myself without you,
Never was, never will be.

Texts I Can't Send

"This isn't healthy"
I'm not giving you the silent treatment
Like you gave to me last weekend.
I'm taking time, just a moment,
To breathe & process &
Remember who I am
Without your dictation
Over what I wear,
What I do,
& who I spend time with.

I am allowing myself
To face the facts,
Really separate my reality
From your dirty laundry
Of words never proven true.

"You don't owe me anything but…"
Stop. You're right.
I don't owe you
Sex or closure or
Protection of your reputation.
You've finally got it right.
I don't owe you anything.

You call me aggressive
Instead of assertive,
One of your favorite words,
& forget that I too have a voice.
A voice to stand up for myself,
A voice you've never heard.
A voice you are going to
Start hearing a lot more often.

Veins

My whole life,
I've refused to get my hopes up.
Because happiness doesn't last
& promises are only ever broken.
I thought I was mature,
A sophisticated young adult
Setting herself up for success.
I abandoned my principles of safety,
Not hoping or wishing for a future,
That's how much I love you.
& I shouldn't have done it.

Because now,
I'm not disappointed in you;
I'm disappointed in myself.
For depending on another
For smiles & warmth,
For letting myself look forward to something
I deep down knew would never be.

I thought everything was relative,
But when the sun fades at the
End of the day & moonlight
Cascades across rooftops,
Nothing is comparable anymore.

Because only longing to be with someone
Three hundred miles distant,
Isn't the same as a plane ticket
From there to here.
Because love isn't enough to fill
My empty veins with blood.

My Person

I used to open my eyes
When my alarm clock screamed
At the ascent of a distant sunrise
& wish I woke up anywhere else
But in my childhood bed
Of tumultuous nightmares
& forgotten memories.

Now I wake up &
Scramble to get dressed,
Throwing off the hug of my covers
Because the faster I move,
The sooner I get to see you.

I used to gaze in the mirror
That's perched crooked
On the bathroom cabinet
& pray that if I blinked once more,
Maybe clicked my heels together twice,
I'd be in anyone's body but my own.

Now I'd stay in my body,
No matter how unsatisfactory,
No matter how uncomfortable,
If it meant you'd hold me a little longer,

If I got just one more of your hugs.
I want to savor the feeling
I have when I'm with you,
Validation in being seen & heard
& loved anyway.

Thank you for being my person.
I owe you the world.